2023 CALIFORNIA DRIVING TEST CHEAT SHEET FOR NEW DRIVERS

DRIVERS PERMIT TEST STUDY GUIDE — BASED ON THE CALIFORNIA DMV HANDBOOK (DRIVING BOOK FOR TEENS)

BRYAN HOLLOWAY

CONTENTS

INTRODUCTION

Congratulations!

The the fact that you have this book in your hands means that you are getting ready to take the California DMV Written Test.

While this is an exciting time, you might also be feeling a little nervous.

Maybe you're wondering what exactly will be on the test, or whether you've studied enough to pass.

All of those feelings are completely normal.

Right now, I want to take a deep breath in and let out a big sigh of relief.

The fact that you have this study guide to help you prepare means that your chances of passing just went up exponentially.

All you need to do now is read through this short study guide and answer the questions at the end of each section.

This study guide is based on the latest edition of the official California DMV Driver Handbook — which is where all the test questions come from.

However, our guide makes the information easy to learn and remember because we've highlighted and summarized the most important points.

You can think of this study guide as the "cheat sheet" version of the California DMV Handbook.

In this book, you'll find everything you need to know for the CA DMV Written Test broken down into bite sized sections that you can read through quickly.

At the end of each section, there are fill-in-the-blank style review questions to help you test your knowledge.

We recommend writing the answers to the review questions in the book or on a sheet of paper (if you prefer) because studies have shown that the act of writing helps you remember information longer.

With that said, let's get dive right into the cheat sheet and get you up to speed for the exam.

We wish you the best of luck on the test!

ALCOHOL & DRUGS

Almost every California DMV Written Test has at least one question about driving under the influence of drugs or alcohol. That's why we put this section first.

Here's what you need to know for the exam:

General Rules

1. It is illegal to drive under the influence of alcohol or drugs. This includes illegal substances, recreational drugs (like cannabis), and prescription medication. It ALSO includes over-the-counter medications like cough syrup and allergy pills, IF they impair your ability to drive.

2. If a police officer suspects that you are under the influence of alcohol or drugs, they can legally make you take a breath, blood or urine test.

3. If you refuse an officer's request to take a test, your driver's license could be suspended or revoked.

4. It is illegal to drink alcohol or use drugs (in any amount) while driving a vehicle.

5. If you are transporting alcohol, it must be sealed in its original container. If the container has been opened, you must put it in the trunk.

Drivers Under 21

There are special rules for drivers under the age of 21.

You cannot have alcohol in the car (even if sealed) unless someone who is 21+ is in the car with you.

If you are caught with alcohol:

1) your car can be impounded for 30 days,

2) you can be fined $1,000,

3) your driver's license can be suspended for 1 year (or delayed 1 year if you don't have it yet.)

If you are under 21, you can be convicted of a DUI if your BAC is 0.01% or higher.

Note: This is DIFFERENT than the BAC limit for drivers 21+.

If you are found guilty of DUI (under 21), you will:

◦ lose your license for 1 year, and

◦ be required to complete a DUI education program

BAC Limits (ages 21+)

The BAC limit for drivers over 21 is different from drivers under 21.

Here are the BAC limits:

(*Make sure you know these for the test.*)

• Under 21: 0.01%

• Over 21: 0.08%

• If you are on probation for DUI: 0.01%

• CDL drivers: 0.04%

• Uber/Taxi/Limo drivers: 0.04%

DUI Penalties

Here's what happens if you are convicted of a DUI in California:

• **First Offense**: License suspended for 6 months, you must complete a DUI program, pay fines, and it stays on your record for 10 years.

• **2 or more offenses**: License suspended or revoked for 2-5 years, you must complete a DUI program, pay fines, and must install and "IID device" on your car.

Medication

If you start taking a new medication, <u>always</u> ask your doctor or pharmacist if it can affect your ability to drive.

It is your responsibility to know how your medications affect your ability to drive safely.

Review Questions

1. For driver's under the age of 21, the BAC limit is

_____.

2. The BAC limit for driver's over the age of 21 is _____.

3. If a police officer suspects that you are under the influence of alcohol or drugs, they can legally make you take a _____, _____, or _____ test.

4. If you are found guilty of a DUI (under 21) how long can you lose your license? _____.

5. In California, DUI convictions stay on your record for _____ years.

Answers:

1. 0.01%

2. 0.08%

3. Breath, blood, or urine test.

4. 1 year.

5. 10 years.

CELL PHONES

Most California DMV Written Tests contain questions about cell *phone use because it is a common cause of car accidents.*

Here's what you need to know for the test:

1. If you're under 18 it's illegal to write, send, or read text messages while driving.

2. If you're over 18, you may operate a cell phone using hands-free voice commands only.

3. It is always illegal for any person of any age to text while driving.

Review Questions

1. Drivers over 18 may operate a cell phone while driving *if and only if* they use a _____.

2. Is it always illegal for drivers under 18 to write, send, or read text messages while driving? _____.

3. Who may legally text while driving? _____.

Answers

1. Hands-free device with voice commands.

2. Yes, it is ALWAYS illegal to text while driving.

3. No one.

DISTRACTED DRIVING

Distracted driving is <u>anything</u> that takes your attention and focus off the road.

Here's what you need to know for the exam:

The 3 types of driver distractions are:

1. **Visual** – eyes off the road.

2. **Cognitive** – mind wandering/not paying attention.

3. **Manual** – hands-off the steering wheel.

Things you should NOT to do while driving:

• use a phone or text

• reach for objects in the vehicle or under your seat

• read

• eat or drink

• put on makeup

Review Questions:

1. The three types of driver distractions are: _____, _____, and _____.

2. Reading while driving is an example of a _____ distraction.

3. Eating while driving is an example of a _____ distraction.

4. Staring at an accident scene while driving by is an example of a _____ distraction.

Answers:

1. Visual, Cognitive, and Manual.

2. Visual.

3. Manual.

4. Cognitive.

DRIVER & PASSENGER SAFETY

Passenger safety rules ensure that everyone in the car stays safe and no one gets hurt. They are also frequently tested on the California DMV Written Test.

Here's what you need to know:

Seatbelts

Seatbelts are the law. You and your passengers must wear a seatbelt anytime you are driving.

The <u>correct</u> way to wear a seatbelt is to place the shoulder strap across your chest and ensure the lap belt is snug across your hips.

Child Passengers

There are special rules for kids.

• Kids under 2 must be secured in a REAR facing car seat in the back seat of a car (not the front seat.)

• Kids under 8 (or less than 4 feet 9 inches) must be secured in a car seat (does not need to be rear facing.)

◦ As a general rule, car seats should be placed in the BACK SEAT of the car.

• Kids over 8+ who are 4 feet 9 inches or taller can use a REGULAR seat belt.

Unattended Children

• NEVER leave kids under 6 alone in a car.

• Kids CAN be left in the car IF there is someone 12+ to supervise.

Hot & Cold Weather

It is dangerous to leave children or pets in a parked car when it is hot or freezing. They can quickly die from heatstroke, hypothermia, or dehydration.

Airbags

You should sit **at least 10 inches** away from an airbag.

If you sit too close, you could be seriously injured if you are in a crash.

Carbon Monoxide

You can reduce the risk of carbon monoxide poisoning by not running the engine in a garage when the door is closed and opening your car windows when you are parked outside with the engine running.

You should also have your exhaust system checked regularly for leaks.

Review Questions:

1. Kids under 2 must be secured in a _____ facing car seat in the back seat of a car.

2. Kids under 8 (or less than 4 feet 9 inches) must be secured in a _____.

3. Never leave kids under _____ years old alone in a car.

4. You should sit at least _____ inches away from an air bag.

5. It is dangerous to leave kids or pets in a car when the weather is too _____ or _____.

6. You and your passengers must wear a _____ anytime you are driving.

Answers:

1. Rear

2. Car seat

3. 6

4. 10

5. Hot or cold.

6. Seatbelt.

CALIFORNIA SPEED LIMITS

There are several speed limits that you need to know for the exam.

Typically, there will be a speed limit sign posted to let you know how fast you are allowed to drive in a given area. However, there are some exceptions.

Here's what you need to know.

California's Basic Speed Limit Law

California's Basic Speed Limit Law says that you *may never drive faster than is safe for conditions REGARDLESS of the posted speed limit*.

School Zones

Unless otherwise posted, the speed limit in an active school zone is **25 mph**.

Blind Intersections

The speed limit when driving through a blind intersection where visibility is reduced is **15 mph**.

FYI: A "blind" intersection has nothing to do with people that are visually impaired.

A blind intersection has no stop signs.

It is often difficult to see in either direction for 100 feet, making it "blind" for you since you cannot easily see if other cars are coming.

Alleys

The speed limit when driving through an alley is **15 mph**.

Railroad Crossings

Unless otherwise posted, the speed limit when driving near or crossing railroad tracks is **15 mph**.

Residential Area

The maximum speed limit when driving through a residential area is **25 mph** unless otherwise posted.

Business Districts

The speed limit in most business districts is **25 mph** unless otherwise posted.

Review Questions:

1. The speed limit in a school zone is _____.

2. The speed limit when driving through a blind intersection is: _____.

3. When driving through a railroad crossing, the speed limit is: _____.

4. The speed limit in a residential district is: _____.

5. The speed limit in a business district is: _____.

6. California's Basic Speed Limit Law says you may never drive _____ regardless of the posted speed limit.

Answers:

1. 25 MPH unless otherwise posted.

2. 15 MPH.

3. 15 MPH.

4. 25 MPH.

5. 25 MPH.

6. Faster than is safe for conditions.

DRIVING SKILLS

This section covers basic driving skills that are commonly covered on the test.

Here's what you need to know:

Managing Space

"*Managing space*" is a *defensive driving skill* where you leave enough room between you and the vehicles around you.

This gives you time to react if another driver swerves or slams on the brakes.

Scanning

When driving, **constantly scan your surroundings** for potential dangers.

Look ahead **10 to 15 seconds**, look to the sides of your car, and check your mirrors often to see what's going on around you.

Tailgating

Tailgating, or following too closely behind the car in front of you, is dangerous because it increases your chances of getting into a crash.

Following Distance

A safe following distance in good driving conditions is **4 seconds**.

Remember to allow more space when the road or weather conditions are not ideal.

Blind Spots

A "*blind spot*" is an area around a vehicle that a driver can't see in their rearview or side mirrors.

You should avoid driving next to other vehicles on the highway. You could be in their blind spot and they may not see you.

Entering the Freeway

You should try to make room for cars entering the freeway *even if* you have the right-of-way.

When entering the freeway, you should drive ***at or near the same speed*** as the flow of traffic

Driving Near Parked Cars

You should not drive too close to parked cars if you can avoid it. They could open their door at any time.

Intersections

When you come to an intersection, you should ***look left, right, and then back to your left again*** before crossing, since traffic coming from the left will be closest to you.

Changing Lanes

Always check to see what is behind you before changing lanes. There could be a vehicle in your blind spot.

Use your mirrors and turn your head to the side and glance back before moving into the lane.

Turn on your signal for *5 seconds* before moving into the new lane. This lets other drivers know what you intend to do.

Stopping

If you are going *55 mph*, you will need *400 feet* of space to come to a complete stop.

If you are traveling *35 mph*, you will need *210 feet* to come to a complete stop.

Note: When driving in poor weather conditions such as rain or fog, it takes longer to stop than when operating in perfect conditions.

Don't Block Intersections

Never block an intersection.

If you come to an intersection with a green light, but traffic is backed up and you don't have enough room to get across, wait to cross until you have enough space.

Backing Up

When backing up, *turn your head* so that you can see through the rear window.

Never rely solely on your backup camera or mirrors.

Signaling

Always use your turn signal when making a turn, changing lanes, or merging on or off the freeway.

If you are planning to make a turn, you should turn on your signal *100 feet before the turn* to let other drivers know that you are slowing down.

Lane Control Lines

If *two solid yellow lines* are separating your lane from the lane traveling in the opposite direction, it means that you are in a NO passing zone.

If the *yellow line* closest to you is *broken*, you may pass if it is safe to do so.

If the line closest to you is *solid*, it means that you may NOT pass.

Two sets of double yellow lines spaced 2-feet apart should be treated as a barrier. You should not drive over them or make a turn across them UNLESS there is a designated opening in the lines.

Solid white lines are used to mark single traffic lanes traveling in one direction, such as one-way streets, alleys, or on-ramps.

Broken white lines are used to separate two or more traffic lanes traveling in the same direction.

If you see *two solid white lines*, this is a lane barrier. You should not leave the lane unless a single broken white line appears.

Driving On Multi-Lane Highways

If you are on a freeway that has three lanes of traffic traveling in the same direction and you wish to pass the car in front of you, you should move into the *left lane* to pass.

The center lane of a multi-lane highway usually has the smoothest flow of traffic.

If you need to drive slower than the flow of the traffic, or if you are exiting soon, you should use the right traffic lane.

HOV Lanes

You can use an HOV or *"high occupancy vehicle"* lane if you have the minimum number of passengers required to enter the lane.

Turn Lanes

You cannot drive more than ***200 feet*** in a center left-turn lane.

Center turn lanes are often shared by traffic going in either direction.

Turnout Areas

You should pull into a *"turnout"* area if five or more vehicles are following closely behind you.

Once the cars pass, you can continue driving on the road.

Bike Lanes

You can ONLY drive in a designated bike lane IF you are parking, entering, or leaving the road.

Shared roadway bicycle markings or *"sharrows"* let you know that bikes can ride in the lane with cars.

Signaling Before a Turn

Use your signal at least ***100 feet before making a turn*** to let other drivers know that you intend to slow down, get into a turn lane, or stop to make a turn.

Turning

If you want to make a left turn at an intersection with a green light that does NOT have a turn lane or an arrow, you should yield to oncoming traffic before making your turn.

If you are turning left from a two-way street onto a one-way street, you should ALWAYS start your turn from the left lane.

If you are turning at a traffic light with a green arrow, you have the right-of-way.

Right Turn On Red

You cannot make a right turn at a red light IF a sign is posted that says, *"No Right Turns On Red."*

If there is <u>no</u> sign prohibiting right turns at a red light, you may turn right after coming to a complete stop and checking for pedestrians or oncoming traffic that could be approaching from the side.

T-Intersections

When turning at a "T" intersection from a one-way street onto a two-way street, you should look for traffic that has the right-of-way.

You may turn right or left from the center lane.

U-turns

You can make a U-turn if it is safe and legal where you are driving.

There should be no vehicles within ***200 feet*** when you start your U-turn.

NEVER make a U-turn at a railroad crossing or when you cannot see **200 feet** in either direction be-cause of a curve, hill, or fog.

Bus Lanes

Passenger vehicles are generally prohibited from driving in bus lanes.

You may only drive in a bus lane if you need to make a turn or cross over the lane.

Passing

As a general rule, you should always ***pass on the left***.

You may pass on the *right side* of a vehicle IF you are on a highway with two or more lanes traveling in the same direction.

When preparing to pass, you should turn on your signal **5-seconds** before moving out of your lane to pass.

You are only allowed to pass *one* vehicle at a time.

Before you return to your lane after passing, use your mirrors to make sure you have enough space.

NEVER pass if you are approaching a hill or curve that limits your visibility of oncoming traffic, or if you are within ***100 feet*** of an intersection, bridge, tunnel, or railroad crossing.

Parking On a Hill

When parking with your car facing *downhill*, turn your front wheels into the curb or toward the side of the road.

When parking with your car facing *uphill*, turn your front wheels away from the curb and let the car roll back a few inches so that the wheels are gently touching the curb.

ALWAYS set the parking brake when you park on a hill, regardless of whether you are facing uphill or downhill. This prevents the car from rolling.

Parallel Parking

When you parallel park, your vehicle should be no more than *18 inches from the curb* or edge of the road.

Pull your car up alongside the space in front of where you intend to park and stop when your rear bumper is in line with the front of the space.

Check your rearview mirror and look over your shoulder to make sure no cars are coming before you begin backing into the space.

Parking At Painted Curbs

You can only park next to a **white** painted curb if you are picking up or dropping off passengers or mail.

You may NOT stop or park in front of a **red** painted curb at anytime.

You can only park in front of a **blue** painted curb if you are disabled and have a special placard or license plate.

No Parking

It is ALWAYS illegal to park:

- If there is a "No Parking" sign,
- In a crosswalk, or
- When you are blocking a driveway, sidewalk, or ramp for disabled persons.

You may never park closer than **15 feet** from a fire hydrant.

You cannot park or stop closer than **7 feet** from a railroad track.

NEVER park your car in the street next to a vehicle parked legally at the curb. This is called *"double parking."*

Any vehicle parked on a California freeway for more than *4 hours* may be removed.

Backing Up

When backing out of a parking space or driveway, turn and look over your right and left shoulders before you start backing up.

Do not rely solely on your mirrors.

Steering

There isn't one right way to steer a vehicle; however, *hand-to-hand steering* and *hand-over-hand steering* are two methods that are recommended.

When driving, place your hands in the *3 and 9 o'clock positions* on the steering wheel.

The only time it is recommended that you steer with *one hand* is when you are backing up.

Using Your Horn

You should only use your horn when it is necessary to alert other drivers to potentially dangerous situations.

Headlights

You must turn your headlights on if it is raining, or if you are driving after sunset or before sunrise.

Switch your high-beam headlights to the low-beam setting when you are within *500 feet* of a vehicle coming toward you.

ALWAYS use your low-beam headlights if you are driving in rain or fog.

It is best to use your high-beam headlights when driving at night on dark or rural roads where visibility is limited.

Any time you turn on your windshield wipers, you should also turn on your headlights.

ALWAYS turn on your headlights when you enter a construction zone.

Emergency Signals

If you see a crash ahead or some other potentially dangerous hazard (i.e., debris in the road), slow down, turn on your emergency flashers and tap your brakes quickly to alert other drivers coming up behind you.

Car Trouble

If you have car trouble while driving on the highway, turn on your emergency flashers and pull off the road as far away from oncoming traffic as possible.

Flow of Traffic

If you drive *faster* than the flow of traffic, you increase your chances of being involved in a collision.

Driving *slower* than the traffic flow or stopping suddenly can be just as dangerous as speeding because other vehicles may swerve to avoid hitting your car. It can also increase your odds of being rear-ended.

Choosing a Lane

If you are driving in the left "passing" lane on a multi-lane highway and notice that cars are passing you on the right, you should move over into the right lane as soon as it is safe to do so to let the other cars pass you on the left.

Curved Roads

It can be difficult to see what's on the road ahead when the road curves.

The inertia or force of going around a curve can pull your car closer to the edge and away from the center of the road, making it easier to lose control of your vehicle, especially when the weather is bad.

Wet Roads

When the road is wet, you should drive *5 to 10 mph* slower than you normally would.

NEVER slam on your brakes if there is water on the road. You could hydroplane and lose control of your vehicle.

Roads are the most slippery right after it starts to rain, especially if it hasn't rained recently. This is because the rainwater mixes with oil and dirt on the road to create a slick surface.

Hydroplaning can occur whenever the road is wet from rain, snow, or a spill. When you hydroplane, your tires lose contact with the road, and you will be riding on top of the water. This causes you to lose traction and makes it very difficult to control your vehicle.

If you start to hydroplane, you should NOT hit the brakes. Instead, take your foot off the gas pedal and allow the vehicle to slow down gradually.

Snow & Ice Covered Roads

When the road is covered with snow, *reduce your speed by half.*

When the road is icy, you should slow down to a crawl.

Windy Conditions

When it is windy, pay special attention to large vehicles driving near you, like semi-trucks and campers, since they can be moved easily by the wind.

Fog & Smoke

When heavy fog or smoke reduces visibility, AVOID driving if you can, or pull over until the fog lifts.

If you must drive, turn on your emergency flashers, go slowly, and use extra caution.

When visibility is reduced, you should increase the distance between you and the vehicle in front of you.

Flooded Roads

If you come to a flooded road, turn around and look for an alternate route.

NEVER drive through a flooded area if you can avoid it.

Flooded roadways can be life-threatening because it can be difficult to tell how deep the water is.

If you drive through water, your brakes could get wet. This can cause them to fail. After going through the water, test your brakes immediately before you continue to drive.

Handling Skids

If your vehicle starts to skid on the road, do not hit the brake.

Instead, take your foot off the accelerator and *turn the wheel in the direction of the skid* until you regain control.

Drifting Off Road

If your vehicle drifts off the pavement, gently tap the brake to slow down gradually.

Check behind you and to your sides to ensure no cars are coming, then gently steer your vehicle back onto the road.

Accelerator Malfunction

If your accelerator (gas pedal) malfunctions or becomes stuck, stay calm and shift the car into neutral.

Apply the brakes to slow down and look for a place to pull over.

Do NOT turn off the engine while the vehicle is moving.

NEVER reach down to look for objects on the ground while the car is moving.

Brake Malfunction

If your brakes are not working correctly, shift the car into neutral and turn on your emergency flashers to alert other drivers that your vehicle has a problem.

Let the car slow down gradually and guide it to a safe spot off the road as soon as you can.

Review Questions

1. A *defensive driving skill* where you leave enough room between you and the vehicles around you is called _____.

2. When driving, **constantly scan your surroundings** for _____.

3. *Tailgating*, or following too closely behind the car in front of you, is dangerous because:_____.

4. A safe following distance in good driving conditions is _____ seconds.

5. The area around a vehicle that a driver can't see in their rearview or side mirrors is called a

_____.

6. When entering the freeway, you should drive _____ as the flow of traffic.

7. When you come to an intersection, you should look _____, _____, and _____ again before crossing.

8. Always check to see what is _____ you before changing lanes.

9. If you are driving **55 mph**, you will need _____ feet of space to come to a complete stop.

10. If you are planning to make a turn, you should turn on your signal _____ feet before the turn to let other drivers know that you are slowing down.

11. If *two solid yellow lines* are separating your lane from the lane traveling in the opposite direction, it means that you are in a _____ zone.

12. If the *yellow line* closest to you is *broken*, you may _____ if it is safe to do so.

13. **Two sets of double yellow lines spaced 2-feet apart** should be treated as a _____.

14. You cannot drive more than _____ feet in a center left-turn lane.

15. You may turn right at a red light if there is no oncoming traffic and _____.

16. How many vehicles are you allowed to pass at one time? _____.

17. When parking with your car facing **downhill**, turn your front wheels _____ the curb or side of the road.

18. When parking with your car facing **uphill**, turn your front wheels _____ from the curb and let the car roll back a few inches.

19. ALWAYS set the _____ when you park on a hill, regardless of whether you are facing uphill or downhill.

20. When you parallel park, your vehicle should be no more than _____ inches from the curb or edge of the road.

21. You can only park next to a **white** painted curb if

_____.

22. When are you allowed to park near a red painted curb? _____.

23. If you drive _____ than the flow of traffic, you increase your chances of being involved in a collision.

24. When the road is wet, you should drive _____ than you normally would.

25. If your vehicle starts to skid, you should turn your wheel _____ until you re-gain control.

Answers

1. Managing space.

2. Potential dangers.

3. It increases your chances of getting into a crash.

4. Four.

5. Blind spot.

6. At or near the same speed.

7. Left, right, and left again.

8. Behind.

9. 400.

10. 100.

11. No passing.

12. Pass.

13. Barrier.

14. 200.

15. If there is no sign prohibiting "right on red" turns.

16. 1.

17. Toward.

18. Away.

19. Parking brake.

20. 18

21. You are picking up or dropping off passengers or mail.

22. Never.

23. Faster.

24. 5 to 10 MPH slower.

25. In the direction of the skid.

CALIFORNIA DRIVING LAWS

In this section we'll cover a number of California driving laws that you may encounter on the exam.

Here's what you need to know:

Insurance & Registration

All vehicles must be registered and insured to drive on public roadways in California.

Headlights

If you are driving *after sunset* or *before sunrise*, you must turn on your low-beam headlights.

It is against the law to leave your <u>high-beam</u> head-lights on when you are approaching another vehicle.

You are required by law to turn on your <u>low-beam</u> headlights when you enter a road construction zone.

School Buses

If a school bus stops ahead of you and turns on its flashing red lights, you are legally required to stop and wait until the lights stop flashing before you continue to drive.

Law Enforcement Stops

If a police car turns on its siren behind you, turn on your right turn signal to let the officer know that you see them and that you intend to stop.

Next, look for a safe place to pull over.

When an officer is approaching your vehicle for a traffic stop, roll down your window and place your hands on the steering wheel or in your lap so that the officer can see them.

Traffic Tickets

If you are issued a traffic citation, you must appear in court if you wish to dispute the ticket, or you must pay a fine.

If you ignore a ticket by failing to show up to court or pay your fine on time, your license can be suspended.

Collisions

Even if you are involved in a minor collision, you must stop to check on the other driver and exchange information.

If you are involved in a collision where someone is injured or killed, you must make a written report to the police **within 24 hours.**

If you are involved in any collision, you (or someone on your behalf) must inform the California DMV within **10 days** of the event.

Driving Record

In California, traffic violations stay on your driving record for at least **36 months.**

"*Points*" are issued on your driver record when you are convicted of a traffic violation or are at fault in a collision.

Drivers who receive four points on their record in one year, or six points in two years are considered to be "*negligent drivers*" by the State of California.

Smoking

It is against the law in California to smoke inside a car when there are minors or children present.

Headphones

It is illegal to wear headphones or earplugs in both ears when driving because you cannot hear what is happening around you.

Transporting Items

It is illegal to transport any items that block your view of the road or to the sides of your vehicle.

Seatbelts

California law requires all passengers to wear a seatbelt when they are riding in a moving car.

Bike Lanes

You can only drive in a bike lane if you are within **200 feet** of a cross street where you plan to turn right.

You may NOT drive in a bike lane at any other time.

Flaggers

If there is a person directing traffic, you should follow their instructions at all times, even if they conflict with existing signs or signals.

Crosswalks

It is illegal to park your vehicle in any crosswalk, whether marked or unmarked.

Blocking An Intersection

It is ALWAYS illegal to block an intersection.

Review Questions

1. All vehicles must be _____ and _____ to drive on public roadways in California.

2. If you are driving _____ or _____, you must turn on your low-beam headlights.

3. It is against the law to leave your _____ headlights on when you are approaching another vehicle.

4. If a school bus stops ahead of you and turns on its flashing red lights, you must _____.

5. If you are issued a traffic citation, you must _____ if you wish to dispute the ticket.

6. If you are involved in a collision where someone is injured or killed, you must make a written report to the police within _____ hours.

7. If you are involved in any collision, you must inform the California DMV within _____ days of the event.

8. In California, traffic violations stay on your driving record for at least _____ months.

9. It is against the law in California to smoke inside a car when there are _____ present.

10. It is _____ to park your vehicle in any crosswalk, whether marked or unmarked.

11. When are you allowed to block an intersection? _____.

Answers

1. Registered and insured.

2. After sunset, before sunrise.

3. High-beam.

4. Stop and wait until the lights stop flashing before you continue to drive.

5. Appear in court.

6. 24

7. 10

8. 36

9. Minors or children.

10. Illegal.

11. Never.

SHARING THE ROAD

Large Trucks

It takes large trucks *longer to stop* than smaller passenger vehicles.

If you slow down or stop quickly in front of a large truck, it could cause a collision.

Do NOT drive alongside a large truck unless you are passing. Tractor-trailers have bigger blind spots than regular cars. They may not be able to see you.

When long vehicles *make turns*, the back wheels have *a shorter path* than those in the front. This causes them to have to swing out wide when turning.

Safety Zones & Bus Stops

If you come to a safety zone where people are boarding or exiting a bus or trolley, you must stop and wait until all pedestrians are safely away from the road before you proceed.

Railroad Crossings

Busses and trucks transporting *hazardous materials* must ALWAYS stop before crossing railroad tracks, regardless of whether there is a stop sign or signal.

NEVER stop on the railroad tracks for any reason.

When approaching a railroad crossing, look AND listen for oncoming trains.

NEVER assume there will be a signal or gate to warn you of an oncoming train.

Stop *at least 15 feet* (but no more than 50 feet) from the nearest railroad tracks when crossing devices, such as lights, are active or blinking.

Emergency Vehicles

When an emergency vehicle is using their siren, you must pull over to the shoulder of the road and stop to give them room to get through.

NEVER stop in an intersection if an emergency vehicle is coming because they may need to make a turn.

NEVER follow an emergency vehicle to their destination.

It is illegal to drive within ***300 feet behind*** any emergency vehicle when its siren is on.

Horse Drawn Vehicles

When driving near horse-drawn vehicles, use extra caution because the driver could lose control of the animal.

Motorcycles

When driving behind a motorcycle, ***keep a 4-second following distance.*** This way, if the motorcycle stops suddenly or skids, you have a better chance of avoiding a collision.

Bicycles

When passing a cyclist, you should *leave at least 3 feet of space between you and them* to avoid knocking them off their bike.

Pedestrians

NEVER pass a vehicle that is stopped at a crosswalk. Someone could be crossing the street that you are not able to see.

If you come to a crosswalk where pedestrians are waiting to cross, stop before you reach the crosswalk and let them pass.

ALWAYS look for pedestrians who may be approaching the crosswalk or intersection before making a right turn.

Intersections

Not all intersections require ALL cars to stop.

Some intersections have a 4-way stop, while others have a 2-way or 1-way stop.

If you come to an intersection with a *4-way stop*, that means all cars must stop at the intersection.

If two cars arrive at the intersection at the same time, the car on the right gets to go first.

Roundabouts & Traffic Circles

When approaching a roundabout or traffic circle, yield to any pedestrians or cyclists crossing the road.

Yield to any vehicles that are already in the roundabout before entering.

Entering the Freeway

When merging onto a highway or freeway, oncoming traffic has the right-of-way.

The ideal speed for merging onto a highway or freeway is ***at or near the flow of traffic.***

Funeral Processions

If you encounter a funeral procession, wait for the procession line to pass before driving.

Constructions Zones

When driving through a construction zone, obey the posted speed limit and *increase your following distance* in case the car ahead of you slows or stops suddenly.

Disabled Vehicles

If you see a vehicle stopped on the side of the road, the best thing to do is to slow down and move over into the left lane if you can. If you cannot change lanes, use extra caution when passing.

Review Questions

1. Tractor-trailers have bigger _____ than regular cars, making it more difficult for them to see you.

2. Busses and trucks transporting _____ must ALWAYS stop before crossing railroad tracks, regardless of whether there is a stop sign or signal.

3. When is it okay to stop your vehicle on a railroad track? _____.

4. When approaching a railroad crossing, look AND _____ for oncoming trains.

5. When an emergency vehicle is using its siren, you   must

_____.

6. It is illegal to drive within _____ feet behind any emergency vehicle when its siren is on.

7. When driving behind a motorcycle, keep a _____ second following distance.

8. When passing a cyclist, you should leave at least _____ feet of space between you and them to avoid knocking them off their bike.

9. If two cars arrive at an intersection at the same time, the car on the _____ gets to go first.

10. When driving through a construction zone, obey the   posted   speed   limit   and
_____ in
case the car ahead of you slows or stops suddenly.

Answers

1. Blind spots.

2. Hazardous materials.

3. Never.

4. Listen.

5. Pull over to the shoulder of the road and stop to give them room to get through.

6. 300.

7. Four.

8. Three.

9. Right.

10. Increase your following distance.

TRAFFIC SIGNALS

Traffic Lights

STEADY RED LIGHT — means STOP before the painted white line on the pavement.

FLASHING RED LIGHT — treat this as a ***stop sign***.

STEADY RED ARROW — this means STOP, do not turn until the light changes to green.

STEADY YELLOW LIGHT — this is a warning light that lets you know that the traffic signal is about to turn red.

FLASHING YELLOW LIGHT — means proceed with caution.

A GREEN LIGHT— means you can drive through the intersection if it is clear.

STEADY GREEN ARROW — you may turn in the direction of the arrow.

When traffic signal lights are **not** working, they should be treated as a STOP sign.

Pedestrian Signals

Walk Sign - This signal light is shown when it is safe for pedestrians to cross the intersection.

It may show the word "walk" in white letters or have an image of a person walking.

Don't Walk - This signal lets pedestrians know that it is not safe to cross the intersection and that they must wait for the signal to change before proceeding.

The signal light will show a solid raised hand with the words "Don't Walk."

Warning - When a pedestrian signal is FLASHING the raised hand symbol or the words "Don't Walk," this is a warning that the traffic light is about to change.

Lane Control Signals

Some highways have special signals over the lanes.

They are often used at:

- toll booths,
- multi-lane highways,
- bridges, and
- tunnels.

Here's what they mean:

GREEN ARROW - When you see a green arrow over a traffic lane, it means you CAN use the lane.

STEADY RED X - if you see this light over a traffic lane it means that you are NOT allowed to use the lane.

STEADY YELLOW X - This signal lets you know that the direction of the lane is changing soon. Move into another lane as soon as it is safe to do so.

STEADY WHITE ONE-WAY LEFT-TURN ARROW
- if you see this arrow over your lane it means that
you may only turn left if you are in that lane.

STEADY WHITE TWO-WAY LEFT-TURN ARROW
- you may ONLY turn left if you are in this lane.
However, this lane is also used by left-turning
drivers who are approaching from the opposite direction.

Review Questions

1. A steady red light means _____ before the
painted white line on the pavement.

2. A flashing red light should be treated as
_____.

3. A green arrow over a traffic lane means
_____.

4. A steady red X over a traffic lane means
_____.

5.   A   flashing   yellow   light   means
_____.

6. If a traffic light is NOT working, what should
you   do?
_____.

Answers

1. Stop.

2. A stop sign.

3. You can use the lane.

4. You may not use the lane.

5. Proceed with caution.

6. Treat it like a stop sign.

ROAD SIGNS

In this section you'll find our road sign reference guide. These signs tell you what to do when you're out on the road, like stopping or yielding.

They also let you know about road conditions, speed limits, or other hazards.

Some of these signs will probably be familiar to you or self-explanatory. But make sure you spend extra time reviewing any that you don't know, because road signs commonly appear on the California DMV Written Test.

When you come to an intersection with a STOP sign you must stop completely.

4-Way Stops

Some intersections have stop signs placed in all four directions. This means that traffic coming from any direction must stop at the intersection.

1 or 2-Way Stops

Some intersections only have stop signs for one or two directions (for example, north and south) while traffic going east and west does NOT have to stop.

If you have a stop sign, but oncoming traffic does not, you must stop and wait for all traffic to clear before entering the intersection.

When you see a YIELD SIGN you must slow down and check for oncoming traffic.

If there is NO oncoming traffic, you do NOT have to stop.

If there is oncoming traffic, you must stop and wait for it to pass before proceeding.

These signs are posted at one-way streets and ramps entering or exiting a highway.

If you see this sign, do NOT enter the street or ramp in the direction you are driving.

When you see a one-way traffic sign it means that vehicles are only allowed to travel in the direction the sign is pointing.

Do not drive the wrong way down a one-way street, ramp, or lane.

Speed limit signs let you know the **maximum speed** you are allowed to drive on the road you are traveling on.

Keep in mind that **California's Basic Speed Limit Law** says that you should NEVER drive faster than is appropriate for conditions, regardless of the posted speed limit.

This sign lets you know that the road you are on intersects with a divided highway.

A *divided highway* is two, one-way lanes that are separated by a median or guide rail.

This sign lets you know that large trucks and tractor trailers are not allowed to use the road or drive on the highway.

This sign lets you know that bicycles are not allowed to ride on the road or highway because it is not safe for cyclists to travel on.

This sign lets you know that people are not allowed to cross the intersection on foot. They must go to another intersection where crossing is permitted.

This sign lets you know that you cannot make a U-turn.

A U-turn is when you make a 180-degree turn to go in the opposite direction.

This sign lets you know that right turns are prohibited at this intersection.

This sign lets you know left turns are not allowed at this intersection.

You cannot park your car in areas where a "no parking" sign is posted.

This sign lets you know that you are in a no passing zone. This means you are not allowed to pass vehicles traveling in the same direction as you.

This sign lets you know that traffic in the left lane must turn left at the intersection. However, traffic in the adjoining lane can turn left or continue driving straight.

This sign lets you know that the center lane can only be used by vehicles that are making left turns in either direction.

This sign lets you know that the roadway splits up ahead. If you are in the left lane, you must turn left. If you are in the right lane, you must turn right.

Make sure that you are in the correct lane depending on which direction you want to travel.

This sign lets you know that you have the option of continuing to drive straight or make a right turn from the lane you are driving in.

This sign lets you know that your lane must turn right at the intersection.

This sign lets you know that your lane must turn left at the intersection.

If you do not want to make a turn, you should move into another lane before you reach the intersection.

This sign lets you know that you need to stay to the right of a traffic island or divider.

These signs are often posted at the beginning of a divided highway.

———

This sign lets you know that a traffic light signal controls right turns at the intersection ahead.

———

This sign lets you know that you may not make a turn in either direction while the traffic light is red.

You must wait for the signal to turn green before proceeding.

This sign lets you know that you can make a left turn at the intersection, but you must yield to on-coming traffic and proceed only when you have enough space to make your turn safety.

This sign means that this is a parking space that is reserved for disabled people.

You must have an authorized license place or placard in order to park in a reserved parking spot.

If you are not authorized to park here, your vehicle may be towed and you will get a fine.

These signs let you know that you are in a school zone.

Slow down and be on the lookout for children.

You must yield to students who are crossing the street.

This type of sign warns you that there is a sharp change in the direction of the road ahead.

The road bends in the direction that the chevron arrow points. Slow down and use caution so that you do not lose control of your vehicle.

This left curve sign warns you that the road ahead veers to the left.

You may need to slow down to stay in your lane as you go around the curve.

This sign warns you that there is a sharp left turn in the road ahead. This is much more severe than a left curve. You should slow down and prepare to turn.

This sign warns you that the road ahead curves to the right. You may need to slow down so that you are able to stay in your lane as you go around the curve.

This sign warns you that the road ahead turns sharply to the right. You should slow down and prepare to turn.

Some signs have a reduced speed limit posted on the sign. You must not go faster than the posted limit when you approach the turn.

This sign lets you know that there is a set of curves in the road ahead.

The road may curve first in one direction, then curve back in the opposite direction.

The direction or shape of the curves will be indicated on the sign.

This sign lets you know that there are three or more curves in a row on the road ahead.

You should slow down and use extra caution until you get through the curves to avoid losing control of your vehicle.

This sign is used to warn you that the road changes at an extreme angle in the direction the arrow is pointing.

Slow down enough that you do not leave your lane as you go around the turn.

This sign warn you that trucks that go too fast around the curve risk tipping or rolling over.

Even if you are not driving a truck, you should be on the lookout for trucks that are driving near you. Give them extra space by slowing down or passing them.

Do not drive beside them while going around the curve. If they rollover or lose control, you could be involved in a fatal collision.

Advisory speed signs are special speed limit signs that tell you the maximum speed you can go when traveling around a curve or turn.

Driving faster than the recommended speed could result in a crash.

Once you pass the curve or turn, you can drive at the normal speed limit again if road conditions are good.

This sign is used to warn you that cars may be merging into your lane from a on-ramp or another roadway.

This sign lets you know that two roadways will meet ahead and travel in parallel lanes.

Traffic from the adjoining roadway does not have to merge since they use a new lane.

This sign is used to warn drivers that they are approaching an area where some traffic is entering the roadway, while other traffic is exiting.

This is often referred to as a "*weave area.*"

This means that many cars may be changing lanes around you and potentially crossing your path.

You should use extra caution in weave areas and pay close attention to what the vehicles around you are doing.

This sign lets you know that you are entering a divided highway.

A divided highway has two one-way roads with a divider or median between them.

You must stay on the RIGHT side of the median when you are driving onto a divided highway.

This sign is used on one-way streets that turn into two-lane roadways.

It lets you know that the one-way street that you are on is turning into a road with two lanes of traffic moving in opposite directions.

You should stay to the right to avoid colliding with oncoming traffic.

This sign is used on roads that have multiple lanes that are traveling in the same direction. It lets you know that the right lane is ending up ahead.

If you are in the right lane, you should turn on your left turn signal and move into the left lane as soon as it is safe to do so.

This sign lets you know that the left lane of a multi-lane roadway is ending.

If you are in the left lane, you should turn on your right turn signal and move into the right lane as soon as it is safe to do so.

This sign lets you know that two roads cross over each other at the intersection ahead.

Crossroads are often 4-way stops, but not always.

Pay close attention to the stop signs at the intersection so that you know who has the right of way if there is no traffic light.

If it is a 2-way stop, traffic crossing the intersection may not have to stop.

This sign lets you know that a road intersects the street you are driving on from one side only.

You should be on the lookout for cars turning onto the roadway from the side road, especially if there is no stop sign or traffic light controlling the intersection.

This sign lets you know that you will need to turn right or left at the intersection ahead.

Stop and look both ways before making your turn, especially if the intersection is not controlled by a traffic light.

This sign lets you know that the road splits into a Y shape with another road intersecting it.

This sign lets you know that there is a traffic circle ahead.

Traffic circles are used to slow down the flow of traffic when there are multiple turns or exits from a single roadway.

When you come to a traffic circle, yield to vehicles that are already in the circle before entering.

Use your turn signal to let other drivers know when and where you plan to exit the circle.

A large arrow that points in both directions lets you know that you must make a sharp right or left turn ahead.

This sign is often placed at the far side of a T-Intersection to let you know that the road does not continue going straight ahead.

This is a warning sign that lets you know that there is a bridge or overpass ahead.

When you approach the bridge or overpass, your lane will become more narrow.

You may need stop and wait before entering the bridge or overpass if there is a large or wide vehicle approaching, as there may not be enough room for both vehicles to pass each other without colliding.

This sign is used to warn you that the road may become very slippery when it rains or snows.

Keep in mind that roads are the most slippery when they first become wet because water mixes with oil and dirt on the road to create a slick surface.

It is very easy for your tires to slip and lose traction if you are driving too fast when this happens.

If the road is wet, slow down and and keep a safe distance from other cars on the road. That way, if you or another driver skids on the roadway, you'll both have more time to react and avoid a collision.

This sign warns you that deer are known to cross in the area. Slow down and drive with caution.

This sign is often posted at or near tunnels, overpasses, or parking garages. It lets you know the structure has a low ceiling.

If your vehicle is taller than the height listed on the sign, you should not enter.

This sign lets you know that the shoulder of the road is lower than the level of the road. In some cases, there could be as much as a 3-inch drop from the road to the shoulder.

This difference can cause you to lose control of your car if one wheel strays onto the shoulder, so use extra caution in these areas.

This sign lets you know that there is a steep hill ahead. You should slow down before going down the hill to stay in control of you car.

Avoid "riding" or overusing your brakes when driving down a steep grade. Rather, tap the brakes periodically to reduce your speed on a hill if you need to.

This sign lets you know that there is a traffic light at the intersection ahead.

You should slow down when you see this sign because there could be a line of vehicles stopped ahead, or the light could be red when you get to the intersection.

This sign lets you know that there is a stop sign ahead.

When you see this sign, slow down and prepare to stop.

This sign lets you know that bicycles frequently cross the road in this area or at this intersection.

Slow down and be prepared to stop to avoid causing injury to a cyclist.

This sign lets you know that there are railroad tracks ahead that you will need to cross over.

You should start looking down the tracks and listening for trains that may be approaching as soon as you see this sign.

This sign lets you know that there is a crosswalk ahead where pedestrians walk.

You should slow down and prepare to stop if any pedestrians are trying to cross the street.

Always look back to your right and check for pedestrians who may be entering the crosswalk before making a right turn. They can be hard to see, especially if you are driving at night.

This sign is used in areas where horse drawn vehicles such as buggies, carts, or carriages are known to use the road regularly.

Try to give these vehicles extra space if you can and use caution when you pass them. Driving too close to horses or honking your horn at them can spook them and cause them to lose control.

Road work signs let you know that there is road construction ahead. If the light on the sign is flashing, that means that it is an active worksite and there may be people working on or near the road.

You should start to slow down and be on the lookout for additional signs or flaggers that may redirect you through the work zone.

Work zone signs let you know when you are entering or leaving an active road construction zone.

Active work zones usually contain more potential hazards that you need to watch out for, such as workers, construction vehicles, and other equipment.

There may also be dust or smoke from the construction that may make it difficult to see clearly.

Always turn on your headlights when you enter an active construction zone and use extra caution to avoid collisions with people or equipment.

When road work is being done, it is common for one or more lanes of traffic to be closed. This type of sign lets you know that the right lane of traffic is closed ahead.

When you see a sign like this, you should turn on your signal and merge into the lane that is open as soon as it is safe to do so.

This sign lets you know that there are people working very close to the road up ahead.

When you see this sign, slow down, stay alert, and use extra caution to avoid hitting or injuring a road worker.

This sign lets you know that there is a human flagger ahead that is directing traffic.

Stay alert and be prepared to stop or slow down. Always follow the flagger's instructions.

This sign lets you know that the road is closed due to flooding. If you see this sign, do NOT drive on the road. Turn around and find another route.

Driving through water on flooded roads is very dangerous and can be life threatening.

Barrels, cones, tubes and panels are often used in road construction zones to direct traffic to an alternate lane or keep traffic out of certain areas.

You should always treat channeling devices like a barrier. Do not drive through them or knock them over. They are there for your safety and the protection of the road workers.

Highway guide signs are used to let you know about upcoming exits to cities or connecting highways and roads.

These signs are usually green with white lettering and will tell you how far away your exit is (i.e. 1 mile)

Highway guide signs that include a yellow "EXIT ONLY" sign with an arrow, let you know that you are in an exit lane. If you stay in this lane, you must exit the highway.

Exits can be on the right or left side of the highway. The placement of the exit number will let you know what side the exit is on. There will usually be arrows pointing in the direction of the exit as well.

Interstate highways are roads that travel through more than one state. These signs are blue and red with white lettering.

Interstates run east to west or north to south. Interstate signs usually say which direction you are heading. For example, the sign in the image lets you know that you are traveling east on I-40.

This type of guide sign lets you know that services such hospitals, food, gas or hotels are available in the area, or they will indicate how far away they are.

These signs are usually blue with white lettering or images.

This type of sign is used to direct drivers to local attractions like state parks, museums, and rest areas. These signs are usually blue, brown or green with white lettering.

Made in the USA
Las Vegas, NV
07 January 2024

84060430R00066